GORDON

BYDAND

Modern Gordon

Ancient Red Gordon

Ancient Dress Gordon

Ancient Old Gordon

CLAN
GORDON

COMPILED BY
Alan McNie

CASCADE PUBLISHING COMPANY
Jedburgh, Scotland

Geneological research regrettably cannot be undertaken by the publisher. A non-profit organization, The Scots Ancestry Research Society, Edinburgh, are able to undertake research for an agreed fee.

Alan McNie, 1980, revised 1983
© *Cascade Publishing Company*
Rowandene, Belses, Jedburgh, Scotland

ISBN 0 9076142 0 5

Page 1 Explanation:
The illustrated tartan is the modern Gordon. The motto on the crest badge means 'Remaining'. In the artist's montage the ancient Gordon clan seat, Huntly Castle (now a ruin) is depicted along with Rock Ivy in the foreground, generally chosen as the clan plant badge.

Gordon Castle, only tower remains of former seat

Gordon Castle

The McIan illustration of Gordon as published (mid-19th century) in 'The Clans of the Scottish Highlands'

CLAN GORDON

Condensed from Keltie's Scottish Highlands (1879)

The Gordons are an ancient and distinguished family, originally from Normandy, where their ancestors are said to have had large possessions. From the great antiquity of the race, many fabulous accounts have been given of the descent of the Gordons. Some derive them from a city of Macedonia called Gordonia, whence they went to Gaul; others find their origins in Spain, Flanders, etc. Some writers suppose Bertrand de Gourdon who in 1199 wounded Richard the Lion-heart mortally with an arrow before the castle of Chalus in the Limoges, to have been the great ancestor of the Gordons. But there does not seem to be any other foundation for such a conjecture than that there was a manor in Normandy called Gourdon. It is probable that the first persons of the name in this island came over with William the Conquer in 1066. The founder of the family came from England in the reign of David the First (1124 - 53) and obtained from that prince the lands of Gordon (anciently Gordun or Gordyn, from the Gailic Gordin, "on the hill"). He left two sons, Richard and Adam, who, though the younger son, had a portion of the territory of Gordon.

The elder son, Richard de Gordon, granted, between 1150 and 1160, certain lands to the monks of Kelso, and died in 1200. His son, Sir Thomas de Gordon, confirmed by charter these donations, and *his* son and successor, also named Thomas, made additional grants to the same monks, as well as to the religious of Coldstream. He died in 1285, without male issue, and his only daughter, Alicia, married her cousin, Adam de Gordon, the son of Adam, the younger brother of Richard above mentioned. The two branches of the family thus became united.

His grandson, Sir Adam de Gordon, Lord of Gordon, one of the most eminent men of his time, was the progenitor of most of the great families of the name in Scotland, In reward of his faithful services, Bruce granted to him and his heirs the noble lordship of Strathbolgie (now Strathbogie) in Aberdeenshire, then in the

Crown, by the forfeiture of David de Strathbogie, Earl of Athole, which grant was afterwards confirmed to his family by several charters under the great seal. Sir Adam fixed his residence there, and gave these lands and lordship the name of Huntly, from a village of that name in the western extremity of Gordon parish, in the Merse, the site of which is now said to be marked only by a solitary tree. From their northern domain, the family afterwards acquired the titles of Lord, Earl, and Marquis of Huntly. Sir Adam was slain fighting bravely in the vanguard of the Scottish army at the battle of Halidonhill in 1333. By Annabella, his wife, supposed to have been a daughter of David de Strathbolgie above mentioned, he had four sons and a daughter. The eldest son, Sir Alexander, succeeded him. The second son, William, was ancestor of the Viscounts of Kenmure.

Sir John Gordon, his great-grandson, got a new charter from King Robert II of the lands of Strathbogie, dated 13th June 1376. He was slain at the battle of Otterbourne in 1388. His son, Sir Adam, lord of Gordon, fell at the battle of Homildon in 1402. By his wife, Elizabeth, daughter of Sir William Keith, great Mareschal of Scotland, he had an only child, Elizabeth Gordon, who succeeded the whole family estates, and having married Alexander Seton, second son of Sir William Steon of Seton, ancestor of the Earls of Winton, that gentleman was styled lord of Gordon and Huntly. He left two sons, the younger of whom became ancestor of the Setons of Meldrum.

Alexander, the elder, was, in 1449, created Earl of Huntly, with limitation to his heirs male, by Elizabeth Crichton, his third wife, they being obliged to bear the name and arms of Gordon. George, the sixth earl, was created Marquis of Huntly by King James in 1599. George, the fourth marquis, was made Duke of Gordon in 1684. George, fifth duke, died without issue in 1836. At his death the title of Duke of Gordon became extinct, as well as that of Earl of Norwich in the British peerage, and the Marquisate of Huntly devolved on George Earl of Aboyne, descended from Charles, fourth son of George, second Marquis of Huntly, while the Duke of Richmond and Lennox, son of his eldest sister, succeeded to Gordon castle Banffshire, and other estates in Aberdeenshire amd Inverness-shire.

The clan Gordon was at one period one of the most powerful and numerous in the north. The clan feuds and battles were frequent, especially with the Mackintoshes, the Camerons, the Murrays and the Forbeses.

The Duke of Gordon, who was the chief of the clan, was usually styled "The Cock of the North". His most ancient title was the "Gudeman of the Bog", from the Bog-of-gight, a morass in the parish of Bellie, Banffshire, in the centre of which the former stronghold of this family was placed, and which forms the site of Gordon castle, considered the most magnificent edifice in the north of Scotland.

Edinburgh Castle, held by Duke of Gordon for one year against William of Orange

Edinburgh Castle

ELGIN CATHEDRAL

Gordon Country
DETAIL MAP OVERLEAF

The map used below and on the following page is intended basically as a pictorial reference. It is accurate enough, however, to be correlated with a current map. The clan boundaries are only marginally correct. No precise boundaries were kept in early times and territories were fluctuating frequently.

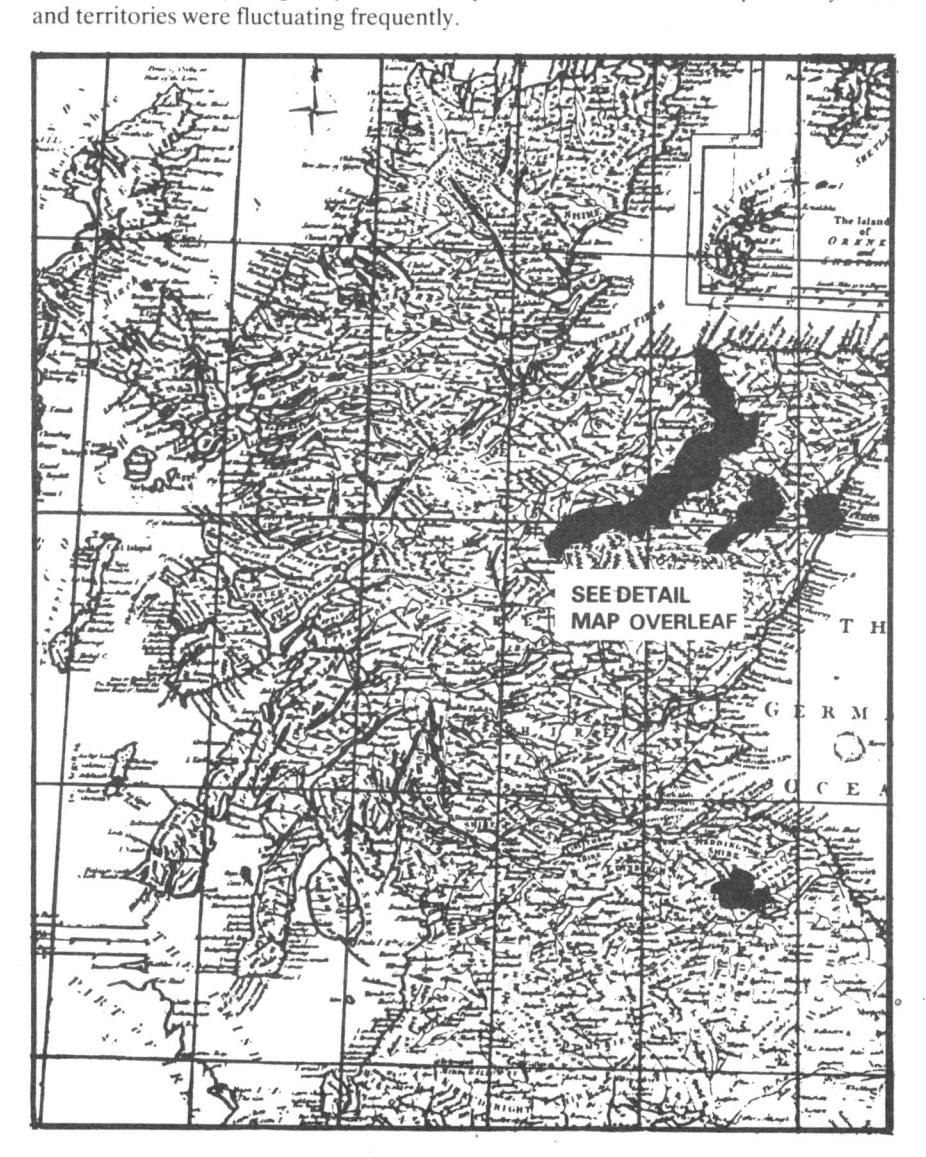

12

Gordon CLAN MAP

GORDON CASTLE (Bog of Gight)

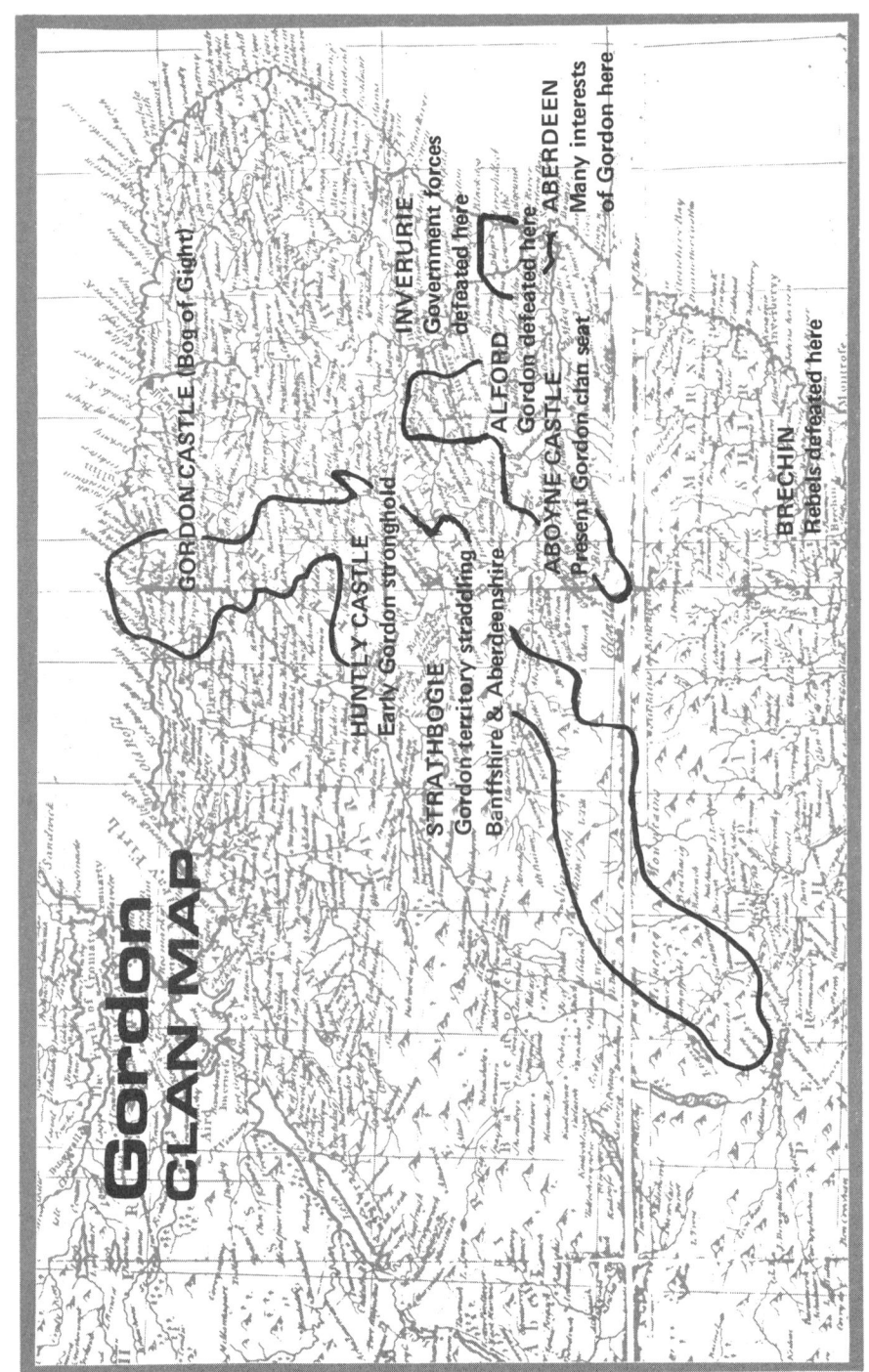

INVERURIE
Government forces defeated here

ABERDEEN
Many interests of Gordon here

ALFORD
Gordon defeated here

ABOYNE CASTLE
Present Gordon clan seat

HUNTLY CASTLE
Early Gordon stronghold

STRATHBOGIE
Gordon territory straddling Banffshire & Aberdeenshire

BRECHIN
Rebels defeated here

Kenmure Castle, Border seat of Gordons

Kenmure Castle

Gordon Associated Names

Associated names have a hazy history. Sometimes they had more than one origin; also clouding the precise location of a particular surname might be that name's proscription or of course a migrant population. Even the spelling of surnames was subject to great variations, shifting from usually Latin or Gaelic and heeding rarely to consistent spelling. In early records there can be several spellings of the same name. Undoubtedly contributing to this inconsistency is the handwriting in official records, which was often open to more than one spelling interpretation.

With regard to the 'Mac' prefix, this was, of course, from the Gaelic meaning, son of. It wasn't long before it was abbreviated to 'Mc' or 'M', until we have reached the position now where there are more 'Mc's' than 'Mac's'.

ADAM, ADAMS, Sir Adam de Gordon was the Clan Gordon founder. Adam sub-prior of Melrose Abbey became abbot of Cupar, 1189. Adam, a witness to charter of lands of Kynemend (Annandale) about 1194 - 1214. Adam, in 1201, was abbot of Newbattle.

ADAMSON Son of Adam. John Adamson of Berewyke, took loyalty oath, 1296. Colin Adamson served as Aberdeen provost, 1340. Cuthbert Adamson was notary public in Glasgow, 1587.

ADDIE, EADIE, EDDIE, EDIE Diminutives of Adam. William Ade of Inverkeithing rendered homage in 1296. Andreas Ade recorded as resident of Edinburgh, 1357. Adam Reid, attendant to King James IV in 1513, called Ade Rede. Salmon Aedie was Aberdeen burgess, 1607. William Aidy, in 1644, served as Marischal College regent, Aberdeen.

AITCHISON, ATKINSON Son of Adam. Aitchison is from diminutive Atty. Atkinson roots from Adkin. Both names originated in East Lothian. John Atkynsoun listed in North Berwick, 1387. John Atkynsoun appears as forestaller, Aberdeen, 1402. Marc Aichesone in shown as a 'custumar' of the Newhavin in Preston, 1590.

AIKEN, AITKEN, ATKIN, ATKINS From Adam, with the suffix 'kin' used and the 'd' of 'Ad' sharpened to 't'. Andrew Atkin, Aberdeen witness, 1469. William Ackin, Brechin witness, 1476. Andree Atkyn, Aberdeen, 1491.

BARRIE From Barrie in Angus. Sometimes confused with Barr, as early spelling 'Barre', is same. Suet Barry, Aberdeen, 1408. John Barry, Aberdeen burgess, 1408. Henry Barry, Glaswegian notary public, 1473

CONNON Diminutive of Conn. Old surname in Aberdeenshire and Banffshire. In 16th-17th centuries, families of this name in Glenbuchat. Followers of earls of Huntly. Took part in battle of Glenlivat, 1594.

CRAIG In earliest records appears in several places, so likely originated in more than one place. For many years a Craig family seated at Craigfintray Castle, near Kildrummie. William de Crag served as an Aberdeen councillor, 1398. Richard de Crag was Dundee vicar, 1443.

CROMBIE This surname has Aberdeenshire origins; derived from Crombie, parish of Auchterless, Aberdeenshire, with the Gaelic 'b' silent and omitted in early spelling and local pronounciation. Robert Crumby was Brechin chapel, 1450. David Crommy, Aberdeen burgess, 1516. Thomas Crommy served as an Aberdeen witness, 1567.

CULLEN From nameplace, Cullen, Banffshire. John de Culane was Aberdeen baillie, 1440. Andrew Coleyn or Colen, listed as Aberdeen merchant, 1438. John of Culane, 'abbot of boneacord', 1486.

DARG, DARGE Likely an English surname. John Darge, North Berwick tenament owner, 1477. Andrew Darg, Aberdeen burgess, 1612. Janet Darge recorded as Dundee resident, 1613. Apparently common surname in Glenlivet.

DORWARD, DURWARD Originally meant door-ward to the king, a very prestigious office. This hereditary post rested with the de Lundins, who migrated to Aberdeenshire. After prolonged dispute they gained large Dee Valley holdings. Alan Durward from this family an important 13th century figure in Scottish history. Thomas de Durward, Arbroath burgess, 1452. John Durewarde was Brechin landholder, 1508.

DUFF From Gaelic Dubh. Duncan Duff served as charter witness at Beauly in 1275. Machaebus Duff, in 1342, was Cullen burgess. Paul Duff recorded in Cawdor, 1414.

ESSLEMONT From name of place in Ellon parish, Aberdeenshire. Andrew Esslemont recorded in Newtown of Damyards of Delgaty, near Turriff, 1760. William Esslemont died in Cottoun of Drumminour, Banffshire, 1829.

GARDINER, GARDNER From occupation. Latin equivalent ortolanus, appears in name of Rogerus Ortolanus, Peebles, 1296. Robert Gardner was notary public in Dunblane, 1426. William Gardennar was Glasgow resident, 1486.

Scottish Roots

The maps below and opposite are intended to show the early occurrence of associated names with clan affiliation. These names also appear with the pertinent historical detail under the associated names on page 14. An historic map has been used as a pictorial background but locations can be fairly easily transposed to a current map.

Gordon ROOTS MAP OF SCOTLAND

Gordon ROOTS MAP OF CLAN COUNTRY

GARRIOCH, GARRIOCK, GARRICK Orkney surname from 1427. That year Henry Garoch was a prominent islander. An Aberdeenshire migrant introduced name variant.

GEDDES From lands of Geddes, Nairnshire. An offshoot family had lands in Kirkurd, Peeblesshire, 1406. Master Matthew of Geddes was a churchman who appeared in the records, 1405. Matthew Geddas, in 1470, served as canon of Aberdeen.

GERRIE Abbreviation of Garrich, etc. Donald Donald Gerrie, condolick, Dunblane resident, 1652. Gerrie recorded in Thursatter, Caithness, 1661.

HUNTLY Originally from Huntlie, Berwickshire. Robert de Hunteleghe, of Roxburghe county rendered homage, 1296. Through Gordon association, Huntly, Aberdeenshire used name with Gordon border association.

JESSIMAN Perhaps from Jesmond, Newcastle-on-Tyne, England. John Jesseman and William Jessieman recorded in Huntly, 1600. James Jessiman, Westertoun, Strathbogie resident, 1654. John Jessieman, Drumdelgie, Moray resident, 1710.

LAURIE, LAWRIE Abbreviations from Lawrence. Edzell church dedicated to St. Laurence, the Martyr. In Stichill, Berwickshire, records of Lauri, 1655 and Laurie, 1665.

MARR Either from place name and surname Mar in Aberdeenshire or Marr, Yorkshire. William de Mar, a witness of grant to Kelso Abbey, 1235. James de Mar in Aberdeenshire, rendered homage, 1296. Richar Mar, in 1302-3, present at St. Andrews inquest.

MAVER, MAVOR From Gaelic maor, a steward in various functions. Name Mavor is from Speyside. John Mawar, Aberdeen witness, 1577. Mark Mawar, Elgin member, Scots parliament, 1593.

MELDRUM From nameplace, Meldrum or Melgedrum, Aberdeenshire, Alexander de Melgedrum, Fife witness, 1278. William de Melkedron, Aberdeen sheriff, 1292.

MILL, MILLS Abbreviation of Miln or Milne. Alexander Myll, mill tenant, Kinrech, Coupar Angus, 1483. John Myl, Arbroath carpenter, 1510. James Mill, Angus-born father of John Stuart Mill.

MILNE, MILNES Common Aberdeenshire name derived from corn-mill. John Myll, dwelling in Aberdeenshire, 1492. Robert Myll, Arbroath witness, 1528. Gilbert Milne witnesses grant of Golspe chaplaincy, 1575.

MOIR From Gaelic, mor, big. An Aberdonian surname pronounced as More. Robertus More was Aberdeen burgess, 1317. Reginald More, Elphinstone witness charter, 1341. John More, Aberdeen canon, 1366.

MORRICE, MORRIS From Maurice, which from Latin Mauricius, moor, a martyred saint, 286 AD. Robert Morse, tenant of bishop of Moray, 1565. James Morriss, Brechin charter witness, 1512. Malcum Morris, Aberdeen burgess, 1559.

TOD, TODD Possibly from designation of fox. Double 't' spelling usual only three centuries back. Baldwin Tod, Landholder, Lambertoun, Berwickshire, 1270. Also appeared in Gordon, Berwickshire, Robert Tod, croft owner, 1280. John Tode, Aberdeen burgess, 1445.

TROUP From nameplace, Troup, Banffshire. Also appeared in Ayrshire, John Troupe, landowner, about 1370-80. Hamund de Troup, Lanarkshire resident, rendered homage, 1296. Hamelin de Troupe, Aberdeen clergyman, 1332.

Second Marquis of Huntly.

List of Emigrants assisted by the Highland and Island Emigration Society, and embarked on board the Ship *Allison* which sailed from *Liverpool* for *Melbourne* on the *13th September* 1852.

Name	Age	Residence	Estate	Remarks
Gordon Alexr	47	Eyre	Ditto	£20.5.0 for family
Mary	46	"	"	
Christy	16	"	"	
Peter	13	"	"	
Margaret	9	"	"	
McKay Alexr	32	Glasphin	MacLeod of MacLeod	£5.0.4 worthy couple
Christy	26	"	"	
Donald	5	"	"	
Marion	3	"	"	
Christy	1	"	"	
Mathieson Mary	24	"	"	sister-in-law of McKay

Some of the clan emigrants who sailed for Australia

Page section courtesy Scottish Records Office

WANDERLUST

For centuries Scots have travelled the globe seeking challenge and fulfilment. A glance through the telephone directories of most countries will uncover Scottish presence. Not so well known are the origins of the Scot. His ancestors came from many diverse places.

About the 6th century Irish settlers from Antrim founded settlements in Argyllshire. These Celtic immigrants, called Scots, provided the nation's name. However they were by no means the only people inhabiting Scotland at that time. For several centuries previously the Picts had controlled much of the northern expanse. These earliest settlers were of unknown origin but they may have come from Sythia.

Also filling in the Scottish mosiac were a branch of the Britons from England who were forced into Strathclyde by some of the Angles. This race, whose name was adopted for England, arrived by the North Sea.

Another race who left their influential stamp on many of Scotland's highest offices were the Normans. From the 8th to the 10th centuries Norsemen extensively raided and settled in the Orkney and Shetland Islands where Norse influences are still highly meaningful today. Other intrepid Norsemen splashed ashore at all parts of the mainland coast with the exception of the south-east.

These races, with their different languages and customs, provided a hetrogeneous mix, which almost miraculously became a Scottish nation, resolute and proud for the most part of their national identity. The melding of the diffuse elements is even more remarkable when it is remembered that the eventual synthesis of Scotland occurred in spite of a formidable linguistic, cultural, economic and geographical divide. The great schism was loosely termed Highlands and Lowlands.

THE SCOTTISH DIVIDE

In fact the Lowlands encompassed the entire east coast of Scotland and penetrated even the most northerly section, the orkney and Shetland Islands. The legitimately-designed Lowland area included all parts of Scotland south of the Forth-Clyde inlets, with all other parts of Scotland categorized as Highland. Gaelic emerged as the language of the Highlands, and Lowland Scots that of the Lowlands.

With Scotland's development as an agrarian economy the geographical divide became a fundamental force in dividing the nation into two widely differing areas of agricultural productivity. The thin soil of the Highlands, coupled with seemingly incessant rain and wind, produced a harsh environment that made even subsistence farming difficult. Contrasting with the hostile environment was the Lowlands, with generally drier weather and fertile soil.

Psychologically the Highlander was inhibited by the tortuous coastline that provided at the time a westward vista to no known promised land. The Lowlanders could fortunately look to a largely hospitable coastline as a base for continental trading. Another advantage for the Lowlands was the ancillary benefits from nearby burghs and institutions, which had limited benefit initially but gathered importance as the centuries passed.

THE CLAN SYSTEM

The Lowlanders had a clan system of their own, with the chief and their landlords sharing a name, but the tenant became increasingly less dependent on the chief for matters such as the maintenance of law and order. The relationship became essentially commercial as time passed. Centralized authority was exercised more easily in the Lowlands, as growing opportunities within the populated areas created a flow from countryside to burgh, which gathered considerable pace with economic change.

Through many harsh centuries the Highlanders functioned within a clan system that generally provided basic humanitarian and economic benefit to tenants, often living in isolated glens. the clan chieftains rented large tracts of land to tacksmen who in turn parcelled the land off to tenants who paid them rent.

Besides agrarian pursuits, the other necessary cog in the clan organizational machinery was a formidable militia. This independent military force mustered the tenants for doing battle against other clans or the English. When attacking other clans they were usually intent on returning with booty. The militia of course had to defend itself against attack.

When law and order became widely enforced through the Highlands, some clans were unable to provide enough food from their meagre soil resources to support all their tenants. The insufficiency provided one spark that would combine with many others to fire the disintegration of the clan system.

THE SCOTTISH MONARCHY

Concurrent with the clan system, and indeed its creator, was the Scottish monarchy, which amazingly survived although beset with several internal and external pressures. The bloody and battered lineage was sustained for many centuries. Pressure to be absorbed into England with its similar language and

Bannockburn

customs would have proved irresistible to many nations. English military thrusts, when successful against Wallace, did not dampen the nationalist fervour of the Scot. That was proven beyond any doubt when, in 1314, Robert the Bruce rallied 10,000 clansmen to an ignominious defeat of the English at Bannockburn. Scottish nationalism still persisted even when Scotland's and England's parliaments were united in 1707.

The parliamentary system gave representation to both countries. Distinctive institutions such as law, church and education were retained, along with a unique cultural heritage. These Scottish elements were buttressed by the canny, quiet resolve of the Scottish psyche that has developed through well over a millenium. Within Scotland today the majority of people consistently want greater automony in managing their own affairs, indicating that the essence of the Scottish identity and self-awareness remains undiluted.

COLLAPSE OF THE CLAN SYSTEM

At the same time as central authority was stabilizing at the beginning of the 18th century, the clan system was, not surprisingly, entering into its death throes. One reason, of course, for disintegration was the declining power of the chief over his clansmen, which was supplanted by other agencies.

Another telling blow was the introduction of sheep into the Highlands. Sheep required far fewer farm workers than cattle, while inexpensively satisfying the needs of burgeoning town populations for food and clothing. The short-lived kelp industry offered only a temporary respite to the rapid depopulation of the destitute Highlands.

Thus the overwhelming defeat at Culloden in 1746 merely brought to a head matters that had been festering for centuries. To wage battle at Culloden, a small force of 5,000 clansmen was mustered when 300,000 people lived in the Highlands at the time. Far more clans were either not represented or fought on the government side.

Following Culloden the already faltering clan system collapsed. This system at its best was a communal attack on a generally harsh environment and unfriendly neighbours. At times it wavered from within, with family feuds fuelled by the proximity and pervasiveness of communal life. Also some chieftains demanded more than a fair share of a meagre lot. Stability was usually maintained, however, through selfless acts of the highest order: the needy were treated with the greatest magnanimity; unrestrained acts of kindness came from every stratum in the clan structure. Today's fascination with clan origins among descendants many generations removed, is usually attributed to a search for identity. But another motivation could be that we live in a world where concern is increasingly for self rather than neighbour. The clan system at its best showed a simple but profound functioning of kith and kin, with care for one another.

ANGLO-SCOTS

The depopulation of the Highlands occurred on a massive scale, with Highlanders, in traditional Scottish fashion, spreading near and far. Some headed for the Lowlands, but for many that proved to be only a stepping stone. For some Scots infected with wanderlust the most important road in Scotland was the road south to England. They believed greater opportunities existed in a more prosperous and populous land. In the first half of the 16th century 3,000 Scots settled in England.

Right through into the twentieth century this flow has been maintained. At times it has reached tidal proportions. Between 1925-35 possibly 60,000 Scots took the road south to England. Over the centuries this brain drain has included Adam Smith, Thomas Carlyle, Sir James Barrie, Robert and John Adam, Arthur Conan Doyle and several British prime ministers.

The Continent has long been a magnet for the wandering Scot. Students for many years have studied there, particularly in France. Some 400 Scottish names were recorded at the University of Paris between 1519 and 1615. Ecclesiastics were also prevalent in Europe. In the 15th century large numbers of Scottish soldiers supported their French friends of the Auld Alliance. Workers of all kinds—merchant seamen, craftsmen, and pedlars—have been recorded in many European countries, with large numbers settling in the Low Countries, particularly Holland.

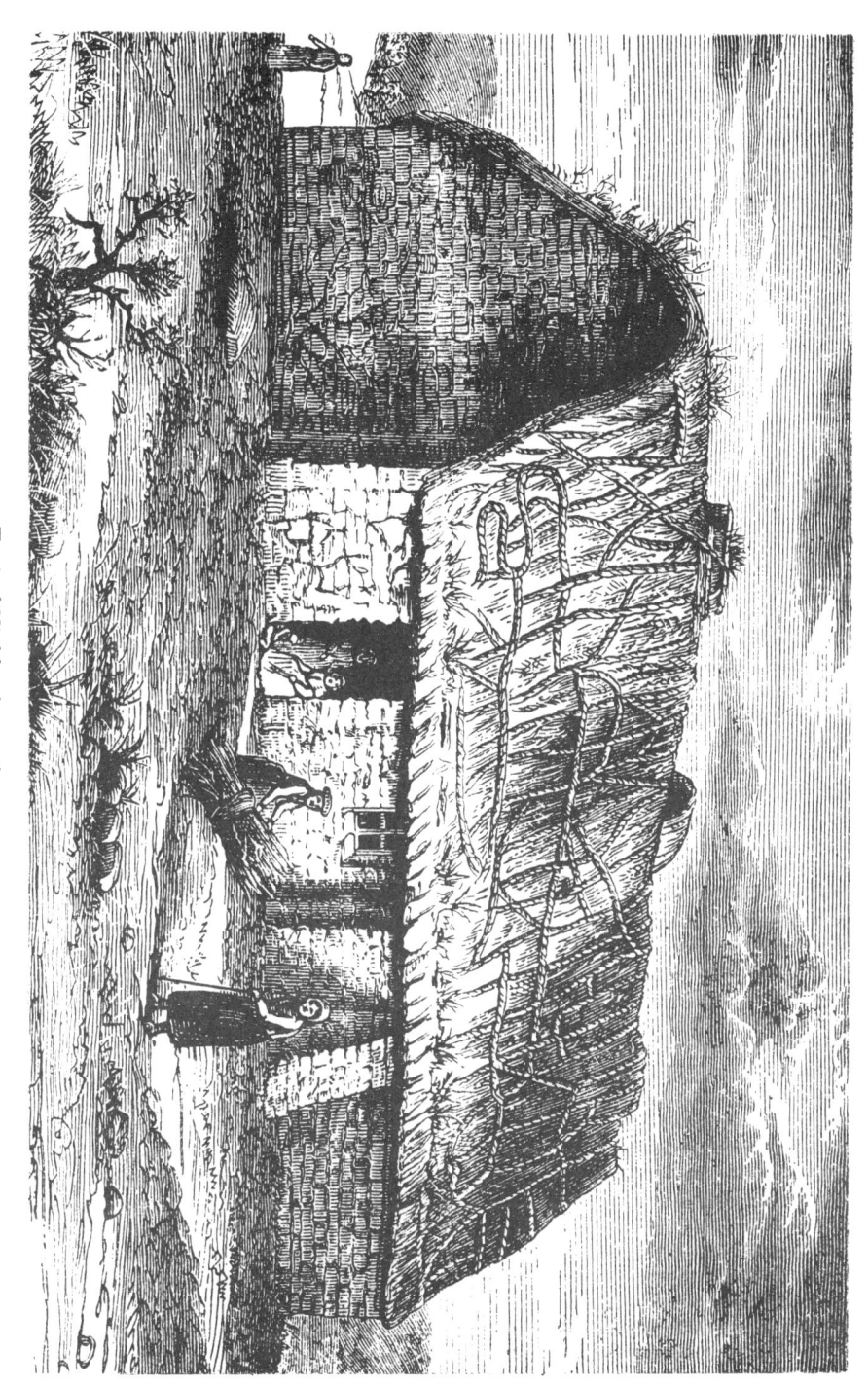

Typical Highland tenant's cottage

Scottish artist David Allan (1744-1796) shows interior of a tenant's period dwelling

SCOTS-AMERICANS

Scots—both Highlanders and Lowlanders—set sail for America in their thousands during the latter part of the 18th century—for the years 1763-75 it could be as high as 25,000. By later standards this was a mere trickle but for that period it could be designated the first immigration wave. Cape Fear Valley in North Carolina, the Mohawk and Upper Hudson valleys in New York, and Attamaha valley in Georgia received the bulk of the Scots.

Even before this large influx some Scots were making notable contributions to their adopted land. Clergyman James Blair founded William and Mary College in 1693. He later became governor of Virginia. Scot Andrew Hamilton was another governor—of New Jersey. John Campbell (1653-1728) was appointed postmaster of Boston, but his real claim to fame was publishing the first newspaper that had been printed in North America, Boston Newsletter (1704).

These three Scots typified the interests of many other emigrant Scots: education, politics and journalism. The exodus from the Highlands was triggered by two other developments, which had considerable bearing on emigration to America. Due to a changed system of Highland land tenure, the tacksmen were being squeezed out. Being resourceful businessmen, they saw an opportunity in America to both organize and lead a settlement. Tenant farmers were also being forced out of the Highlands by huge rent increases.

One sizeable group of Scots should be taken into consideration, particularly at the time of the American Revolution. These were the Ulster Scots, who settled in Northern Ireland in the 17th century. Their descendants accounted for a significant proportion of the 189,000 people of Scottish origin recorded in America in 1790. Their position in the American War of Independence was largely anti-British.

Settlers from Scotland as a whole did not support the revolution and many emigrated to Canada, although there were notable exceptions. John Witherspoon was a framer of the Declaration of Independence. Naturally enough, as an aftermath of the revolution Scottish emigration declined for a few years. However between 1820 and 1950 Scots emigrating to America numbered at least 800,000. Obviously among that number there were those who returned home, but when it is remembered that the population of Scotland did not reach five million until the second quarter of this century, it is a considerable portion. During that period possibly the two most important figures of Scottish birth were Andrew Carnegie and Alexander Graham Bell.

In America as elsewhere the Scots have assimilated well, but nevertheless their heritage has not been forgotten. The staggering proliferation of Highland games, pipe bands, and clan associations across America ensures that the vitality and appeal of the Scottish tradition will be nurtured by Scots and their descendants for years to come.

Gordons and their descendants have long played a prominent part in American life. Among the notables was John Gordon (1832-1904) whose grandfather came from Ayrshire, Scotland. He was probably the most important military figure in Georgia's history. Following distinguished service in the Confederate army he subsequently became US senator for seven years and governor of Georgia for four years.

SCOTS-CANADIANS

The first groups of Scots to arrive in Canada needed indomitable spirit. Those, who arrived as destitute Highlanders in the present-day Maritimes, found little to better their desperate condition. One such group arrived in 1773 at Pictou, Nova Scotia, on the Hector; the plucky passengers waded ashore behind the reassuring skirl of the pipes.

Another wave of Highlanders settled in Upper Canada (Ontario) following the American Revolution. Of particular interest was the Glengarry settlement in the township of the same name, which was settled by many of the Clan MacDonnell of Glengarry, Invernesshire. Members of other clans spread themselves through many parts of Ontario including these notable Scottish areas: Perth, Lanark County; MacNab Township; Guelph; Talbot; Middlesex, Huron and Bruce Counties.

A large number of United Empire Loyalists also arrived in Ontario following the American Revolution, including some of the many Scots who were crown supporters at the time of the revolution. No account of Scottish pioneers would be complete without referring to the heroic and selfless efforts of Lord Selkirk to found an early 19th century Red River settlement (for impoverished Highlanders) in Manitoba. His laudable plans were brutally thwarted several times by traders of the North West Company.

To the east, especially in Ontario, conditions were relatively easier for the rapidly increasing numbers of immigrants from 1815-1850. Ontario was still attracting the lion's share. The Scot, adventurous as ever, continued to form an exceptional percentage of the new arrivals. By 1871 there were approximately 550,000 Scots in Canada, while from vastly more populous England there were slightly over 700,000.

The West was won by settlers at the end of the 19th century and the beginning of the 20th century, with still large numbers of Scots spreading their influence across the prairies. The unique Scottish heritage is alive and well in Canada, with a difference in emphasis between Nova Scotia and the rest of Canada. In Nova Scotia the roots, which are Gaelic, go back much further. Gaelic is still taught at college level on Cape Breton Island. The Scottish traditions of Nova Scotia are based on their Highland heritage. In the rest of Canada the Scottish traditions are wider based, with Burns Suppers, for example, being very popular. Some Scots who have left indelible marks on Canada's path to greatness are: Canada's first prime minister, Sir John A. Macdonald; inventor Alexander Graham Bell; explorer-trader Sir Alexander Mackenzie; publisher-politician George Brown.

Reproduction of drawing by Scottish artist, David Allan (1744-96).

Poor Father of ... Children

David Allan graphically illustrates a major Highland problem: over-population

From earliest days Gordons have contributed significantly to Canadian development. Among the prominent personalities was Sir Arthur Hamilton Gordon (1829-1912) who was the youngest son of the 4th Earl of Aberdeen. He was secretary to his father when he was Prime Minister of Great Britain 1852-1855 and in 1861 Gordon was appointed lieutenant-governor of New Brunswick. He was the author of 'Wilderness Journeys in New Brunswick' in 1846.

SCOTS-AUSTRALIANS

The first flood of emigrants to Australia were convicts, who were sent between 1788-1820 to New South Wales and Tasmania. Among these convicts were political as well as criminal prisoners. Some of the political prisoners were 18th century reformers, who had corresponded with French revolutionaries. Today such persons could well be members of parliament or clergymen. And among the criminal prisoners were probably those who were improperly convicted as well as those who had committed a petty crime.

It should be stated that sometimes Scottish political convicts were allowed to manage their own farms or pursue a trade. Free settlers, enticed by the large fertile parts of Australia being opened, quickly changed the large proportion of convicts compared with free settlers. By 1828 those who chose to emigrate to New South Wales numbered 4,673, compared with 7,500 freed convicts and 15,600 still in bondage. The number of free settlers had more than quadrupled in nine years. One of the earliest free settlers was Robert Campbell (1769-1846) who was a Sydney merchant in 1798. Two successive Scottish governors—Lachlan Macquire and Sir Thomas Brisbane—may have helped Scottish emigration.

Scots were prominent in further expansion in the 1830s, this time in Western Australia with the Swan River Colony. Another Scot, Angus MacMillan founded the Grippsland area, ideal for grazing. Further advancement was made in Queensland by Scot, Thomas Petrie, who opened up this area. In Victoria, Scottish farmers succeeded in a big way. Massive acreages for raising cattle and sheep were owned by many Highlanders, who became very wealthy. Neil Campbell, for example, claimed that within two years of arriving from Mull in 1838, he earned £1000 per annum.

The discovery of gold in New South Wales and Victoria created a dramatic upturn in Scottish emigration to Australia. For those who didn't strike it rich, farming was still expanding at an amazing rate; ancillary employment associated with gold mining also triggered thousands of jobs.

Scottish strength in Australia is exemplified by the 100,000 Scots reported there at the turn of the century. Two Scottish descendants achieved Australia's highest office: Prime Ministers Sir Robert Gordon Menzies and (John) Malcolm Fraser, with Mr Fraser preferring his Scottish given name. Particularly strong Scots-Australian traditions are pipe bands and Scottish country dancing.

R. R. McIan's Victorian illustration from 'Clans of the Scottish Highlands'. Although bound for Canada, the rueful appearance of this emigrant could apply to any destination. Some emigrants, sailing in squalid conditions, failed to reach their new homeland alive and those that did often encountered formidable difficulties.

Australian affairs have been shaped by Gordons for many generations. Among the notables was Sir John H. Gordon (1850-1923) who was born in Kilmacolm, Scotland. A successful solicitor, he was elected to the legislative council for the Southern District and for much of that time held cabinet office. Sir John was then raised to the Supreme Court bench.

SCOTS-NEW ZEALANDERS

With the purchase of huge parcels of land in 1839, the New Zealand Land Company paved the way for large scale settlement of New Zealand by British immigrants. Between 1839-44, a large number of Scots were aboard the 63 boats that landed from Britain. Getting an early start were 150 Scots who landed at Port Nicholson, on the extreme south coast of the North Island. Other Scots spread out to many other parts of New Zealand. Included in those settlers were a doctor and an engineer, neither of whom followed their profession but elected to become sheep farmers, which provided ample financial compensation.

Otago, in the southern part of the South Island, was to have a Free Church of Scotland settlement organized on a very rigid basis. As with other overly-controlled overseas settlements they encountered many difficulties. As part of the settlement plan the tower of Dunedin was founded. Today the Scots influence there remains on the street signs, with many of Edinburgh's most famous street names found there. The discovery of gold in 1861 in Otago brought in the 'gold rush brigade', which provided a short-term spur to the economy.

But long-term prosperity was found by farming in Otago as well as many other parts of New Zealand. Successful farming, of course, boosted the whole economy, which in turn produced thousands of jobs. Many of these were filled by Scots emigrants in the latter part of the 19th century. By 1901 there were 48,000 Scots living in New Zealand, compared with 110,000 English, proportionately a much larger Scottish presence than English. New Zealand today maintains many Scottish traditions, with particular emphasis on Caledonian societies and an exceptionally large number of pipe bands.

Perhaps Scotland's most famous son was Peter Fraser, who was born (in 1884) in Fearn, Ross and Cromarty, of humble origin. From 1940 this dedicated Prime Minister guided New Zealand through the demanding wartime and postwar period.

The Gordons have frequently played a leading role in New Zealand's growth. One prominent contributor was Sir Arthur H. Gordon (1829-1912) son of the 4th Earl of Aberdeen. A Liberal MP he was also private secretary to William Gladstone. Several colonial appoints then preceded his designation as governor of New Zealand in 1880. This able administrator encountered difficulty with cabinet ministers who wanted a populist hard line against the Maoris. He left the governship in 1882 after having other policy differences.

The best loved of many Scottish traditions observed world-wide is surely the singing of Auld Lang Syne, notable at Hogmanay (New Year's Eve), but also on many occasions when Scots and those of any other nationality familiar with Burns famous adaptation are gathered together in good fellowship.

ACKNOWLEDGEMENTS
We are indebted to staff members of the Hawick Library and Scottish Room, Edinburgh City Libraries for their generous assistance. Research work done by Barbara Blackburn has proved valuable and thorough.